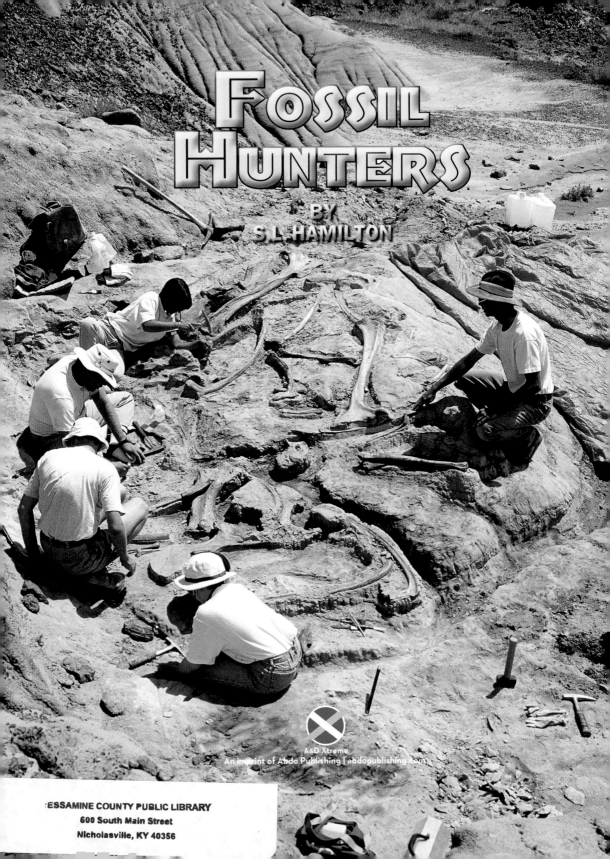

FOSSIL HUNTERS

BY
S.L. HAMILTON

A&D Xtreme
An imprint of Abdo Publishing | abdopublishing.com

abdopublishing.com

Published by Abdo Publishing, a division of ABDO, PO Box 398166, Minneapolis, Minnesota 55439. Copyright ©2018 by Abdo Consulting Group, Inc. International copyrights reserved in all countries. No part of this book may be reproduced in any form without written permission from the publisher. A&D Xtreme™ is a trademark and logo of Abdo Publishing.

Printed in the United States of America, North Mankato, MN.
102017
012018

Editor: John Hamilton
Graphic Design: Sue Hamilton
Cover Design: Candice Keimig and Pakou Vang
Cover Photo: iStock
Interior Photos & Illustrations: Alamy-pgs 8-9, 10-11 & 22-23;
AP-pgs 12-13, 14-15, 17, 20-21, 24-25, 27 (bottom) & 28; Glow Images-pg 1;
iStock-pg 32; Minden Pictures-pgs 2-3; Reuters Pictures-pgs 18-19;
Royal Tyrrell Museum-pg 29 (bottom); Shutterstock-pgs 4-5 & 30-31;
Wikimedia Commons-pgs 7 (inset), 26, 27 (top) & 29 (top);
Yale Peabody Museum/Division of Vertebrate Paleontology-pgs 6-7;
The Natural History Museum-London-pg 29 (middle).

Publisher's Cataloging-in-Publication Data

Names: Hamilton, S.L., author.
Title: Fossil hunters / by S.L. Hamilton.
Description: Minneapolis, Minnesota : Abdo Publishing, 2018. |
    Series: Xtreme Dinosaurs | Includes online resources and index.
Identifiers: LCCN 2017946716 | ISBN 9781532112959 (lib.bdg.) |
    ISBN 9781532150814 (ebook)
Subjects: LCSH: Paleontology--Juvenile literature. | Prehistoric
    animals--Juvenile literature. | Dinosaurs--Juvenile literature.
Classification: DDC 560--dc23
LC record available at https://lccn.loc.gov/2017946716

Contents

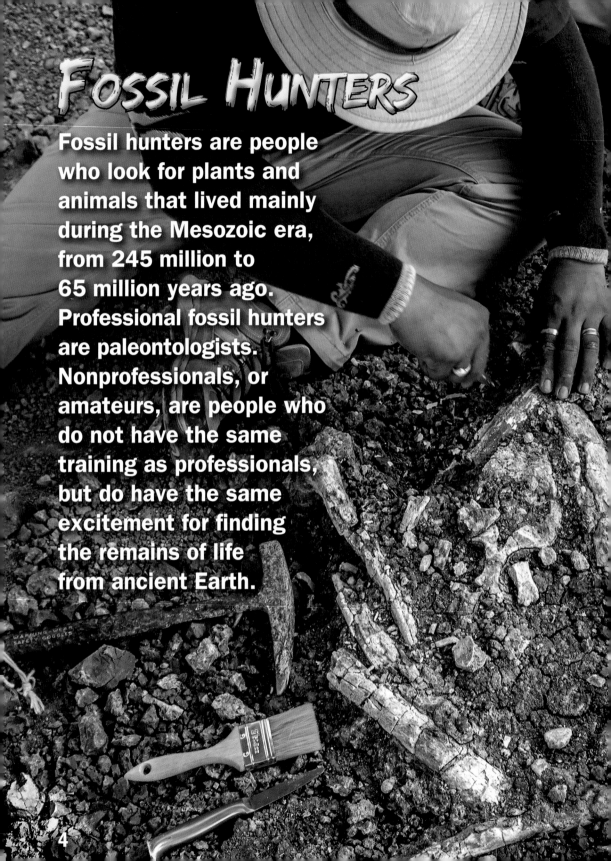

FOSSIL HUNTERS

Fossil hunters are people who look for plants and animals that lived mainly during the Mesozoic era, from 245 million to 65 million years ago. Professional fossil hunters are paleontologists. Nonprofessionals, or amateurs, are people who do not have the same training as professionals, but do have the same excitement for finding the remains of life from ancient Earth.

XTREME FACT – Paleontologists sometimes study just one form of ancient life. For example, scientists who study only flying reptiles are called pterosaurologists. Micropaleontologists study fossils so small they must be viewed with a microscope. Paleobotanists study fossil plants. Geologists study rocks and the fossils in them.

HISTORY

People studied ancient fossils as early as 500 BC. In 1822, editor Henri Marie Ducrotay de Blanville came up with the French term "paleontologie." Over time, the scientific field became known as "paleontology."

One of the most well-known fossil hunters was England's Mary Anning. She earned money by selling her dinosaur discoveries. In the early- to mid-1800s, she found ichthyosaur, plesiosaur, and pterosaur fossils. People were fascinated with ancient life. The world of fossil hunting became popular.

Mary Anning

Torosaurus (Perforated Lizard) The skull was collected by Othniel C. Marsh around 1914.

XTREME FACT – American paleontologists Othniel C. Marsh and Edward Cope fiercely competed with each other from 1877 to 1892. Their efforts to find fossils became known as "The Bone Wars."

PROFESSIONALS

People go to college to become paleontologists. They study biology, or the science of living creatures. Today's animals give paleontologists clues about prehistoric living things.

Lumbar vertebrae

Rib

Pelvis

Rib

Caudal vertebrae

Fe

Paleontologists study geology. They learn what kinds of rocks contain fossils, such as limestone. They learn what various fossil bones look like. They are taught how to put the bones together to recreate ancient animals. They learn foreign languages since fossil digs are all over the world.

AMATEURS

Amateur fossil hunters are self-trained people interested in finding ancient plants and animals. Because there are so many amateurs, they sometimes discover new and existing species that may never have been found. They advance science with their finds.

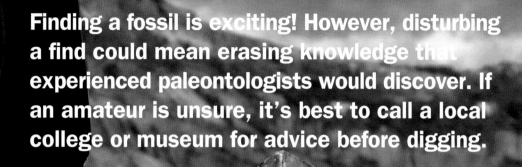

Finding a fossil is exciting! However, disturbing a find could mean erasing knowledge that experienced paleontologists would discover. If an amateur is unsure, it's best to call a local college or museum for advice before digging.

XTREME QUOTE – *"Enjoy looking at everything on the ground around you. Look at the little things, the big things, and everything in between."*
—Ray Stanford, amateur fossil hunter whose fossil finds have been placed in the National Museum of Natural History, Smithsonian.

WHERE TO LOOK

Look for fossils in sedimentary rocks. These are rocks made up of many layers such as shale, limestone, and sandstone. Quarries are popular sites for finding fossils. However, it's important to always get permission to explore on private property.

XTREME FACT – There are 22 states in the continental United States with fossil parks. It is illegal to take fossils from these protected sites. However, visitors learn what to look for when searching for fossils elsewhere.

Fossil hunters need equipment to take care of themselves and their finds. Since fossils are often found in hot, dry areas, it is important to carry water and wear sturdy footwear and a hat or hard hat (if going into a quarry). They also need safety glasses, knee pads, a map or GPS, rope, and a bright safety vest or jacket.

Paleontologists dig up the vertebra of a sauropod dinosaur after it was uncovered while workers were digging a pipeline in Wyoming.

Equipment includes a backpack or carrying bag, shovel, hammer, chisel, steel picks, probes, soft brushes, magnifying glass, and a sieve or strainer. Once fossils are uncovered, they must be carefully excavated and then transported. Fragile fossils are sometimes glued to keep them from breaking. Individual plastic bags, padded boxes, as well as foam wrapping with elastic bands can protect them.

A field kit from the Natural History Museum of Utah includes:

1) Chisel
2) Walkie-Talkie
3) GPS
4) Rock Hammer

5) Probes & Chisels
6) Brushes
7) Swiss Army Knife, Fork & Spoon

8) Vinac (a dissolvable glue-like bead coating for fragile fossils)
9) Markers & Plastic Bags
10) Tape Measure

BONE OR STONE?

It is sometimes difficult to tell if a find is a bone or a stone. After all, fossils are the remains of living things transformed into rock. Experienced fossil hunters look at three clues:

1. Color. Does the item's color differ from the rock surrounding it? If so, it may be a fossil.

2. Texture. Are there patterns on the item? Bones have a sponge-like interior. It can be seen on a cross section.

3. Shape. Bones, as well as fossil teeth, shells, and other ancient living things, all have unique shapes. A fossil will likely have a shape unlike the rest of the rock surrounding it.

XTREME FACT – Some fossil hunters use a "tongue test" to see if an item is a fossil. Since bones are porous (containing holes), if the piece sticks to your tongue, it may be a fossil. Soil and rock don't usually stick.

A dinosaur leg bone found in a rock shows the differences between it and the surrounding stone.

Color

Shape

Texture

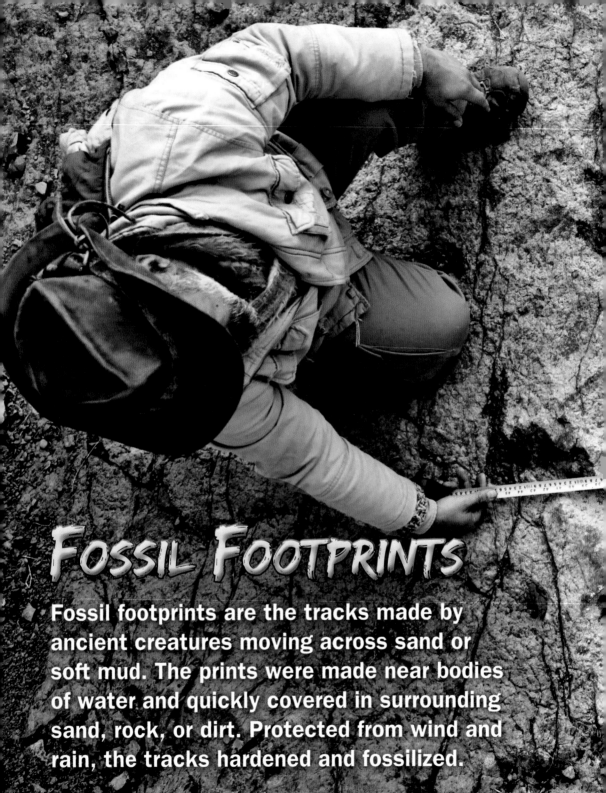

FOSSIL FOOTPRINTS

Fossil footprints are the tracks made by ancient creatures moving across sand or soft mud. The prints were made near bodies of water and quickly covered in surrounding sand, rock, or dirt. Protected from wind and rain, the tracks hardened and fossilized.

Fossil hunters have found these footprints around the world. Many prints have surfaced in dry areas of South America, the western United States, Australia, and Mongolia. Fossil hunters can walk in the steps of dinosaurs.

XTREME FACT – Fossil footprints are called "trace fossils." They are physical proof of activities of extinct creatures. Trace fossils also include tail drags, trails, bite marks, poop, burrows, eggs, and nests.

COPROLITE

Fossilized poop is called coprolite. The word comes from the Greek *Kopros Lithos,* or "dung stone." Coprolites do not smell, and look very much like rocks, but are poop shaped.

Trying to figure out which prehistoric creature pooped is difficult. Paleontologists look at the scat of modern creatures to help them identify the pooper. They also look at the contents of the coprolite. If tiny bone fragments are found, they know it came from a carnivore. They also look to see if there are specific ancient animals in the area. If so, it's likely the poop came from one of them.

XTREME FACT – People who study prehistoric poop are called "paleoscatologists."

Fossil Eggs & Nests

Dinosaurs, like modern reptiles, laid eggs in nests on the ground. Only a few dinosaur nests and eggs have been found by fossil hunters. It is very difficult to tell what prehistoric animal laid the eggs.

Paleontologists may guess what laid the eggs by their size and shape. They also check for other fossils in the area. Sometimes a few hatchlings are found with the eggs. Scientists may perform CT scans or 3-D x-rays to help identify the egg. Scientists may even break open an egg to look at the contents.

FOSSIL PLANTS

Plants grew all over prehistoric Earth. Finding them is usually much easier than finding fossil bones.

Like animal fossils, plant fossils are found in sedimentary rock. Fossil hunters use pickaxes and shovels to dig through layers of dirt. Once one leaf is found, there are often many more in the same area.

XTREME FACT – Paleobotanists, people who study fossil plants, use their knowledge of prehistoric flora to discover more about dinosaurs and other ancient creatures that lived in Earth's early environment.

FAMOUS FOSSIL FINDS

For hundreds of years, people have made amazing discoveries of prehistoric Earth. Paleontologists and amateur fossil hunters continue uncovering great fossil finds.

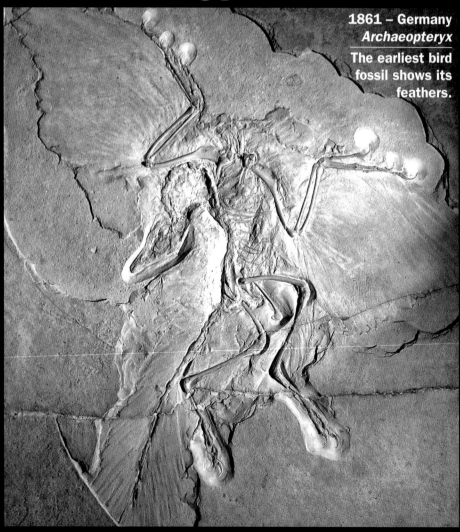

1861 – Germany
Archaeopteryx

The earliest bird fossil shows its feathers.

1971 – Gobi Desert, Mongolia
Protoceratops and *Velociraptor*

Dinosaurs fighting before being buried in a landslide.

1996 - New Mexico
Hadrosaur

Skin fossil from a duck-billed dinosaur showing incredible details.

Rubber Mold

Original Fossil

1990 – South Dakota
Tyrannosaurus rex

"Sue" (named after the finder, Susan Hendrickson) is the largest and most complete *T. rex* fossil ever found.

1994 – Gobi Desert, Mongolia
Citipati - Oviraptor

"Big Mama" sits on her nest of eggs.

1800s – Germany
Stenopterygius

An ichthyosaur mother was buried while giving birth.

2011 – Alberta, Canada
Nodosaur

An incredible fossil with skin and armor details.

GLOSSARY

CT SCAN
Computerized axial tomography is a type of x-ray that gives a cross-section image of the item being scanned.

EXCAVATE
To remove dirt, rock, and other natural materials in a careful and exacting way in order to find buried remains.

FLORA
All the plants living in a certain area or time period. Paleobotanists study the flora of prehistoric Earth.

GEOLOGY
The study of rocks to develop an understanding of the history of Earth.

GPS (GLOBAL POSITIONING SYSTEM)
A system of orbiting satellites that transmits information to GPS receivers on Earth. Using information from the satellites, receivers can calculate location, speed, and direction with great accuracy.

Hatchling
A newborn that has just hatched from its egg.

Mesozoic Era
A time in Earth's history from about 245 million to 65 million years ago. Dinosaurs roamed the Earth at this time. This overall era includes the Triassic, Jurassic, and Cretaceous periods.

Quarry
A place where different types of stone are mined for use as building materials. Limestone, a whitish rock, is made up of the deposited remains of ancient marine animals and other minerals. Many excellent fossil finds have been discovered in limestone quarries.

Sedimentary Rock
Rock that is formed by a slow process of pressing together small bits of sand, mud, and pebbles over millions of years. This rock often has the fossil remains of ancient plants and animals.

Online Resources

Booklinks
NONFICTION NETWORK
FREE! ONLINE NONFICTION RESOURCES

To learn more about Xtreme Dinosaurs, visit abdobooklinks.com. These links are routinely monitored and updated to provide the most current information available.

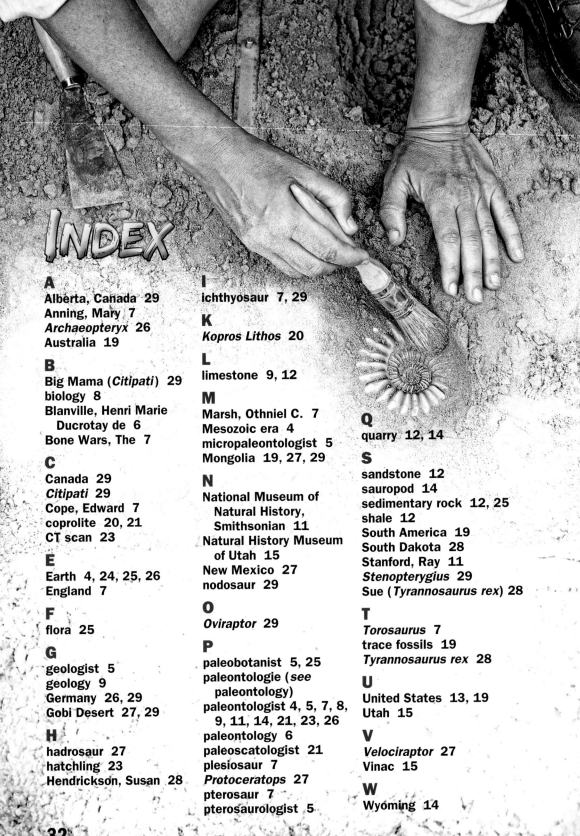

INDEX